Martin Luther King, Jr.

Civil rights leader Martin Luther King, Jr., photographed in 1967.

JUNIOR ■ WORLD ■ BIOGRAPHIES

Martin Luther King, Jr.

KATHY KRISTENSEN
LAMBERT

CHELSEA JUNIORS

a division of CHELSEA HOUSE PUBLISHERS

Chelsea House Publishers

EDITOR-IN-CHIEF   Richard S. Papale
MANAGING EDITOR   Karyn Gullen Browne
COPY CHIEF   Philip Koslow
PICTURE EDITOR   Adrian G. Allen
ASSISTANT ART DIRECTOR   Howard Brotman
MANUFACTURING DIRECTOR   Gerald Levine
SYSTEMS MANAGER   Lindsey Ottman
PRODUCTION COORDINATOR   Marie Claire Cebrián-Ume

JUNIOR WORLD BIOGRAPHIES

SENIOR EDITOR   Kathy Kuhtz

Staff for **MARTIN LUTHER KING, JR.**
COPY EDITOR   Christopher Duffy
EDITORIAL ASSISTANT   Danielle Janusz
PICTURE RESEARCHER   Sandy Jones
SERIES DESIGNER   Marjorie Zaum
COVER ILLUSTRATION   Daniel Mark Duffy

9 8

Library of Congress Cataloging-in-Publication Data
Lambert, Kathy Kristensen.
   Martin Luther King, Jr./Kathy Kristensen Lambert
   p.cm.—(Junior world biographies)
   Includes bibliographical references and index.
Summary: A biography of civil rights leader Martin Luther King, Jr.
ISBN 0-7910-1759-1
1. King, Martin Luther, Jr., 1929–1968—Juvenile literature. 2. Afro-
Americans—Biography—Juvenile literature. 3. Civil rights workers—
United States—Biography—Juvenile literature. 4. Baptists—United
States—Clergy—Biography—Juvenile literature. [1. King, Martin Luther,
Jr., 1929–1968. 2. Civil rights workers. 3. Clergy. 4. Afro-Americans—
Biography.] I. Title. II. Series.
E185.97.K5L28 1992   91-34986
323'.092—dc20   CIP
[B]   AC

Contents

Martin Luther King, Jr., (center) talks with reporters on the steps of the Montgomery County Courthouse in March 1956. King was on trial for organizing a boycott of Montgomery's segregated buses.

1

The Bus Boycott

On December 1, 1955, a small black woman named Rosa Parks waited for a bus in Montgomery, Alabama. After finishing her day's work as a seamstress, she had gone to do some shopping. Tired and carrying packages, she was eager to get home and rest. When the bus finally came, she was delighted to find a seat in the first row behind the section marked Whites Only.

Each time the bus stopped, more and more

white people got on, until every seat was taken. When two more white men got on, the driver told the first row of black people to give up their seats and stand in the back of the bus. Three of the four people got up, but Rosa Parks did not move. The driver shouted at her, "Look woman, I told you I wanted that seat. Are you going to stand up?"

Rosa Parks knew that the law required blacks to sit in the back of the bus and to stand up if a white rider needed a seat. But she refused to move. The driver found a policeman, who arrested Rosa Parks and took her to jail.

The next day E. D. Nixon, a leader in the Montgomery chapter of the *National Association for the Advancement of Colored People* (*NAACP*), called Martin Luther King, Jr., a 26-year-old Baptist minister, and told him about the arrest of Rosa Parks. "We got our case!" he said.

The NAACP had been waiting for a chance to challenge the *segregation* laws in force throughout the South, which required the separation of blacks and whites. Besides limiting where blacks could sit on a bus, the law kept them from using the same drinking fountains, sinks, rest rooms, swimming pools, hotels, and restaurants used by whites. Blacks had separate entrances and seating areas in theaters and baseball parks. Black children were not allowed to go to school with white children or use the same playgrounds. If a black person met a white person on the sidewalk, the black was expected to move aside and let the white pass by. When blacks went to a white's home, they were expected to use the back door.

These acts of *discrimination* were called *Jim Crow* laws, and the NAACP believed the time had come to put an end to these unjust laws by challenging them in court. The arrest of Rosa Parks gave them the opportunity. E. D. Nixon also suggested to King that the blacks should refuse to ride on the city buses, an action known as a *boycott*. King was not sure that a boycott would work. One reason he had doubts about the boycott was that the black community had never organized anything like it before. But King's friend and fellow minister, Ralph Abernathy, called him and persuaded him to join the boycott.

The next day, a black organization known as the Women's Political Council handed out leaflets urging blacks to stay off the buses on Monday, December 5, when Rosa Parks was to go on trial. The leaflets said, "If we do not do something to stop these arrests, they will continue. The next time it may be you, or your daughter, or your mother. Don't ride the buses to work, to town, to school, or anywhere on Monday."

King and his wife, Coretta, were up early on December 5. There was a bus stop in front of their home on South Jackson Street. They were anxious to see how many black people would be on the 6:00 A.M. bus, which was always crowded. Their goal was to have the buses only half-full. Martin was in the kitchen pouring some coffee when Coretta called from the window, "Come quickly—it's empty!" The Kings watched in amazement as three buses rolled by, all empty except for the driver.

King got into his car and drove around the city. Every bus he saw was nearly empty. Black people were going to work in taxis and car pools, or they were walking. King even saw one man riding on a mule. Altogether, he counted only eight blacks riding on buses that morning.

At 9:00 A.M. hundreds of blacks were at the Montgomery courthouse to support Rosa Parks. The judge found Rosa Parks guilty of violating the state segregation law and fined her $10 plus court costs. Her lawyer appealed the decision to a higher court, which later ruled in her favor.

Encouraged by the success of the boycott, the black leaders formed the Montgomery Improvement Association (MIA). They selected Martin Luther King, Jr., to be their president. When he was asked if he would accept the position, he said, "If you think I can render [give] some service, I will." He had not been in Montgomery very long, and he thought the people would prefer a leader who was older and better known. When he was asked to speak to the group after his selection, he was unprepared. He usually practiced his *sermons* for church until he had them memorized. So he went into his study and prayed for God's help.

When King reached the church where the MIA was meeting, 1,000 people were crowded inside. Another 4,000 people filled the streets. King began his speech by talking about Rosa Parks's case. Then he said, "There comes a time when people get tired. We are here this evening to say to those who have mistreated us so long, that we are tired. Tired of being segregated and humiliated; tired of being kicked about by the brutal feet of oppression [the act of treating someone harshly or cruelly]. Love must be our regulating ideal. . . . We must not become bitter. . . . If you will protest courageously, and yet with dignity and Christian love, when history books are written

Rosa Parks appears in court with civil rights leader E. D. Nixon (center) and attorney Fred Gray. Rosa Parks's refusal to give up her seat to a white man led to the Montgomery bus boycott.

in future generations, the historians will have to pause and say, 'There lived a great people, a black people, who injected new meaning and dignity into the veins of civilization.' This is our challenge and our overwhelming responsibility."

The crowd enthusiastically applauded King's 16-minute speech. There was no doubt in their minds that they had chosen the right person to lead their challenge.

For the next 12 years, Martin Luther King, Jr., led the fight for *civil rights* throughout the South. He believed that it was "never too late to do what was right" and that problems should be solved by using nonviolent forms of protest, such as the Montgomery bus boycott. He did not seek power and influence; people came to him because his ideals inspired blacks to work for full legal, social, and economic equality. As King often told his friends, "History has thrust something on me which I cannot turn away."

The house on Auburn Avenue in Atlanta, Georgia, where Martin Luther King, Jr., was born in 1929. The house belonged to his grandparents, who were important members of Atlanta's black community.

2

Growing Up
in the South

Martin Luther King, Jr., was born on January 15, 1929, in a bedroom in his grandparents' home at 501 Auburn Avenue in Atlanta, Georgia. His parents were Martin (Michael) Luther King, Sr., a Baptist minister, and Alberta Williams King, a former teacher. They had originally named him Michael, after his father. But his father later changed both of their names to Martin Luther, in honor of the 16th-century German religious reformer.

Alberta King's father, Adam Daniel Williams, was the pastor of Ebenezer Baptist Church and was active in black political organizations as well as the local chapter of the NAACP. After Martin, Sr., and Alberta got married in 1926, Adam Williams hired his son-in-law as his assistant. When Williams died suddenly in 1931, Martin, Sr., took over as pastor of Ebenezer Baptist Church.

When Martin, Jr., was born, the Kings were living with his Grandma Williams. Grandma Williams was very fond of Martin. She could not stand to see him spanked. When he was punished, she always had a hug, a kiss, or a kind word to ease the pain. Martin adored her and called her Mama.

Martin had an older sister, Willie Christine, called Christine, and a younger brother, Alfred Daniel. One day when he and Alfred were roughhousing, Alfred slid down the banister of the front stairs and knocked Mama down. When she did not stand up, Martin was sure that he and Alfred had killed her. He felt that he could not face life without her. Crying hysterically, he ran up to his room and threw himself out the window, falling 12 feet to the ground. His parents rushed outside, shouting to Martin that Mama was alive, just a little shaken. After hearing this news, Martin, unhurt, got up and walked away.

A few weeks later, Martin sneaked out of the house to watch a parade that he knew his father would not have allowed him to see. When he returned home, he learned that his grandmother had died of a heart attack. Feeling guilty for having been at the parade, Martin once again rushed upstairs and jumped out the window. Again he came away without any serious injury, but he cried and pounded the ground in grief over the loss of Mama.

Martin grew up during the *Great Depression*, a period in the 1930s when many people lost their jobs and were poor. The Kings, however, owned their own home and had an automobile. Martin did not have to leave school and go to work like many children did. But he did understand the value of a dollar and delivered newspapers to earn extra money.

Martin spent many hours at the Ebenezer Church, listening to his father preach and singing in the choir. But he did not always behave like an angel at home. He once hit his brother over the head with a telephone and knocked him out. His sister claimed that when it was time to do the dishes, Martin always seemed to be in the bathroom. Once, when Martin's mother wanted all of her children to learn to play the piano, Alfred decided to break the piano with a hammer. But Christine and Martin persuaded him to loosen the legs of the piano stool instead. When the music teacher came and sat down at the piano, the stool collapsed, and the teacher fell to the floor. When Martin's father heard about this prank, he gave each child a whipping that Martin remembered as "simple, quick and persuasive."

Martin enjoyed reading, and he was such a good student that he skipped grades in both elementary school and high school. He was well mannered in class and liked playing sports, especially football.

At an early age, Martin learned the pain of racial discrimination, which means to judge someone negatively because of the color of his or her skin. When he was five, he often played with a white boy whose father owned the neighborhood grocery store. One day, when he went to play with the boy, the boy's parents told Martin to go away and not come back again. Martin did not understand. They told him he could not play with their son anymore because "We are white and you are colored."

Hurt and confused, Martin went home and told his mother what the white people had said. She stopped what she was doing and spent several hours explaining the blacks' history of slavery and the laws of segregation. She told him, "You must never feel that you are less than anybody else. You must feel that you are *somebody*."

Martin's father put those words into action.

One day, he took Martin to the store to buy some shoes. The shoe salesman told Martin's father that he would help them if they sat in the black section of the store. Mr. King said, "There's nothing wrong with these seats. We're very comfortable here." When the salesman insisted that they move, Martin's father became angry and said, "We'll either buy shoes sitting here or we won't buy shoes at all." As they were leaving the store without the shoes, Mr. King told Martin, "I don't care how long I have to live with this system, I will never accept it."

Martin Luther King, Sr., was an inspiring preacher and a man who refused to accept racial segregation.

Martin soon had some of his own experiences with discrimination. At the age of 14, when he was in the 11th grade, he entered a speaking contest sponsored by the Negro Elks Society. The contest took place in Dublin, Georgia, and Martin traveled there by bus with his teacher, Mrs. Bradley. Martin's speech, which was titled "The Negro and the Constitution," won first prize.

On the return trip to Atlanta, Martin and Mrs. Bradley had seats in the first row of the black section of the bus. Every seat on the bus had been taken. When some white passengers got on the bus, the driver told Martin and Mrs. Bradley to give up their seats. They did not move quickly enough to suit him, and the driver began swearing at them. Martin did not want to move, but Mrs. Bradley told him they must obey the law. They stood up the remaining 90 miles to Atlanta.

Martin later recalled, "That night will never leave my memory. It was the angriest I have ever been in my life."

Martin Luther King, Jr., (front row, center) listens to a lecture during his final year at Morehouse College. King graduated from Morehouse at the age of 19 and decided to study more before becoming a preacher.

3

Entering the
Struggle

In 1944, when Martin was only 15 years old, he enrolled in Morehouse College, the all-male, all-black college in Atlanta that his father and grandfather Williams had attended. Martin's father wanted Martin to continue the family tradition and become a minister. But Martin had mixed feelings. He had grown up in the church, but he was upset by the shouting and stomping that

Dr. Benjamin Mays, a leading minister and one of King's teachers at Morehouse College. Dr. Mays showed King that a preacher could inspire his listeners to work for social change without sounding too emotional.

occurred during worship in some black churches. It embarrassed him. He thought he could better serve others as a doctor or a lawyer.

Martin changed his mind when he got to know Morehouse's president, Benjamin Mays. Mays was a minister who believed in equal rights for blacks. Martin liked his calm and polished style of preaching. Listening to the speeches Mays delivered to the students every Tuesday, Martin decided that a minister could not only inspire people to worship God but could also encourage them to solve social problems.

After three years at Morehouse, Martin told his father that he wanted to be a preacher. Mr. King responded by inviting Martin to preach a sermon at the Ebenezer Church. Martin preached brilliantly, and the congregation felt he would make a great preacher. Martin's father was so moved that he knelt to pray and thank God for giving him such a fine son. On February 25, 1948, Martin was ordained a minister, and his father named him assistant pastor at Ebenezer Baptist Church.

Martin graduated from Morehouse that June and decided to continue his education at Crozer Seminary in Chester, Pennsylvania. Crozer was the first integrated school Martin had ever attended. (To integrate means to allow people of all races to participate.) Most of the students were white, and Martin found that his fellow students liked and respected him. He learned theology, which is the study of religion, and philosophy, which is the study of ideas and principles that guide a person's life. He earned A's in almost all his classes.

While at Crozer Seminary, Martin attended a lecture given by Dr. Mordecai W. Johnson, president of Howard University, a leading black college. Dr. Johnson had visited India, and he told the students about a courageous man named Mohandas Gandhi. Gandhi, who was called Mahatma, which means "great soul," had led India's struggle for independence from Great Britain. King was fascinated to learn that Gandhi believed in the powers of love and *nonviolence* to end oppression. He had led peaceful boycotts, strikes, and marches. India's British rulers found that all their soldiers and guns were useless against people who would neither fight back nor surrender. In 1947, India became an independent nation.

King was so excited by Gandhi's ideas that he ran out and bought a half dozen books on Gandhi and his movement. What he read in those books had a major influence on his leadership of the civil rights movement in the United States.

In June 1951, Martin graduated from Crozer as the top student in his class. He won a scholarship, a grant of money, in the amount of $1,300 to help him continue his education. He used this money to go to Boston University. Martin's father had wanted Martin to come back home and take up his duties at Ebenezer, but he understood his son's desire to go on learning. He even gave Martin a new green Chevrolet as a gift.

In Boston, Martin worked hard, but he also liked to party and go dancing. One day he told a friend, Mary Powell, that he missed the charm of southern women. Mary Powell gave him the phone number of Coretta Scott, a young woman from Alabama who was studying at the New England Conservatory of Music in Boston. King called Coretta and asked her for a date. She agreed

In 1954, the congregation of the Dexter Avenue Baptist Church in Montgomery, Alabama, asked King to be their minister. While he was a minister there, he became a leader of the civil rights movement.

to have lunch with him the next day. When the two met, Coretta was not impressed by Martin and thought that he was too short. But as she talked with him over lunch, she began to be moved by his ideas.

Martin fell in love with Coretta; he even hinted on their first date that he wanted to marry her. He told her that she had everything he wanted in a wife—character, intelligence, personality, and beauty. But Coretta wanted a career as a singer and was not interested in marriage. As she continued to date Martin throughout 1952, she began to fall in love with him.

Martin Luther King, Sr., did not want his son to marry Coretta Scott. He wanted his son to be at Ebenezer and felt that he should marry a young woman from Atlanta. But Martin, Jr., told his mother that nothing would prevent him from marrying Coretta Scott. His father gave in and offered to perform the ceremony. Martin and Coretta were married on June 18, 1953, on the front lawn of the Scotts' home in Marion, Alabama.

Martin was still working on the research paper for his doctor of philosophy (Ph.D.) degree, but he did not have to return to Boston to finish it. He was ready to become a full-time preacher. Coretta tried to convince him to remain in the North, where they would not have to deal with segregation, but Martin believed he was needed most in the South. He also had to decide where to preach. His father was eager to have him at Ebenezer, but Martin now wanted the freedom of having his own church.

At Christmastime, Martin was asked to preach a sermon at the Dexter Avenue Baptist Church in Montgomery, Alabama. The members of the church liked his preaching and invited him to become their minister. He accepted, realizing that a great challenge lay ahead. He knew that segregation was even harsher in Alabama than in Georgia. Montgomery, Alabama, had been the first capital of the Confederacy, the group of 11 southern states that separated from the United States during the Civil War. Any attempt to change the old ways would meet with great resistance in Montgomery.

In May 1954, the U.S. Supreme Court banned segregation in public schools. The states would no longer be allowed to have separate schools for blacks and whites. Angered by this change in the law, many southerners wanted to fight the Court's ruling. Segregationist groups such as the *Ku Klux Klan*, a secret group that insists that the white race is supreme, increased their membership, and the acts of violence against blacks grew.

Encouraged by the Supreme Court decision, King urged his congregation to take a more active role in the fight for integration. He asked them to join the NAACP and to vote in every election. White election officials made it almost impossible for blacks to register to vote.

Election officials required blacks to pass a test of knowledge, called a literacy test, and to pay a tax, known as a poll tax, before they could vote. No whites had to pass a literacy test. King told his followers that they had a duty to overcome these obstacles and that they should not give up until they had succeeded in voting.

Martin and Coretta King pose with their children, Martin III, Dexter, and Yolanda. By 1963, when this photo was taken, the Kings had moved to Atlanta, where Martin took over as minister of his father's church.

4

Victories and Defeats

The year 1955 was an important one for King. On November 17 his daughter Yolanda Denise was born. He earned his Ph.D. degree from Boston University, and he began his close friendship with Ralph David Abernathy, minister of Montgomery's First Baptist Church. The two men had much in common: They both worked for social justice and wanted to put an end to poverty and discrimination. Their friendship was a great source of strength when they had to face problems.

Then, on December 1, 1955, Rosa Parks refused to give up her seat on a Montgomery bus to a white passenger. Rosa Parks's arrest inspired the bus boycott and the founding of the Montgomery Improvement Association (MIA).

As the bus boycott continued, the MIA presented three demands to the bus company: Bus drivers must stop insulting black riders; passengers should be seated on a first-come, first-served basis; and the bus company must hire some black drivers. King believed that the bus company would quickly agree to these demands because the MIA was not urging an end to segregation.

But the bus company did not agree to the changes. The company's lawyer said that if it gave in, blacks "would go about boasting of a victory they had won over white people; and this we will not stand for." The MIA replied that it would not back down from its demands, and the boycott continued.

The MIA organized car pools to replace the buses. Although some of the drivers got lost and cars broke down, the people united and made the car pool system work. As the boycott continued, some of Montgomery's whites turned to terrorism. They made threatening phone calls to King's home, as many as 30 or 40 on a single night. Then, on January 30, 1956, as King was speaking at Ralph Abernathy's church, someone threw a bomb onto the front porch of his home. When King learned what had happened, he rushed home to find everyone at the house frightened but un-

Montgomery women getting out of a church-owned station wagon during the 1956 Montgomery bus boycott. Car pools using vehicles like this one helped make the bus boycott a success.

harmed. A crowd of armed and angry blacks gathered in the street, waiting for the signal to take revenge. But King stuck to his belief that violence accomplished nothing. He urged the crowd to answer evil with Christian love. Hearing his words, the people calmed down and soon went back to their homes.

On February 21, 1956, the city officials tried to break the bus boycott by charging King and about 100 MIA members with violating a little-known state law that forbade boycotts. When King's trial began on March 19, more than 500 blacks packed the courtroom. After three days of testimony, the judge found King guilty and sentenced him to pay a $500 fine or to serve 386 days in jail. King's lawyers appealed the verdict.

In May 1956, a federal court ruled in favor of Rosa Parks and declared that the Alabama law allowing bus segregation was illegal. The city of Montgomery appealed the decision to the U.S. Supreme Court.

In November 1956, the city tried to stop the boycott in court by claiming that the car pools organized by blacks were blocking traffic and that they were creating a public nuisance. This move created a crisis for the MIA. If the city could ban the car pools, they would be able to break the boycott. King later admitted that as he sat in court on November 13, "I was faltering in my faith and my courage."

During a break in the hearing, a reporter came up to King and handed him a slip of paper. When King unfolded the paper he read a news bulletin: The U.S. Supreme Court had declared Alabama's laws requiring segregation on buses to be unconstitutional. After 381 days of peaceful struggle and carpooling, the victory had been won.

A month later, King, Ralph Abernathy, and Rosa Parks waited at the bus stop in front of King's house. When the bus arrived, King got on first and took a seat in the front row. A white man sat beside him.

King's victory in Montgomery was only the beginning of the fight against segregation. In this photo, federal troops break up a crowd protesting the integration of Central High School in Little Rock, Arkansas.

The success of the boycott created a feeling of pride, unity, and accomplishment among the black people of Montgomery. But they knew they still had a long struggle ahead to gain their full civil rights. The segregationists were fighting back, not in the courts but in the streets. On December 28, 1956, a group of whites set fires throughout the city and shot guns at buses. A month later, four black Montgomery churches, including Abernathy's, were firebombed.

King responded to these violent acts by saying, "We will meet your physical force with soul force. We will not hate you, but we will not obey your evil laws."

News of the success of the bus boycott spread, and so did King's fame. In February 1957, *Time* magazine printed King's portrait on its cover. He had become a national celebrity. He received many invitations to speak, job offers, and book contracts, most of which he turned down.

On May 17, 1957, King carried his message

to the nation's capital. On that date, 25,000 blacks and whites gathered at the Lincoln Memorial in Washington, D.C., for the Prayer Pilgrimage for Freedom. President Dwight D. Eisenhower had proposed a law that would give the government the right to investigate racial discrimination and help blacks in the South exercise their right to vote. The marchers came to Washington to urge Congress to pass the bill, making it the law. Many well-known blacks spoke, including King, labor leader A. Philip Randolph, New York congressman Adam Clayton Powell, Jr., and Jackie Robinson, the first black to play major-league baseball. Although Congress passed the Civil Rights Act of 1957, southern congressmen were able to remove the sections of the bill that protected blacks' voting rights. King was disappointed about the final version of the bill but said, "The present bill is far better than no bill at all."

King wanted to organize the entire South to fight for improving civil rights. Impatient with the lack of action by the NAACP, he and his supporters started a new group called the *Southern Christian Leadership Conference (SCLC)*. Working with local churches, the SCLC planned nonviolent actions to *protest* segregation.

While planning the new protest, King wrote a book about his life and the Montgomery bus boycott. *Stride Toward Freedom: The Montgomery Story* was published in 1958. King knew that his position at the head of the civil rights movement would expose him to danger. In September, only a few weeks after the book came out, King went to Blumstein's Department Store on 125th Street in Harlem, New York City's largest black neighborhood, to autograph copies of his book. As he shook people's hands and signed the books, a middle-aged black woman pushed through the crowd, took a seven-inch-long letter opener from her purse, and stabbed King in the chest. King fell back in shock, with the letter opener still piercing his chest. An ambulance rushed him to Harlem Hospital, and surgeons worked for several hours to close up his wound.

When King came out of surgery, the doctors told his family and friends that he would live. The blade of the letter opener had stopped right next to his aorta, the large artery that carries blood from the heart to the rest of the body. If the blade had gone a fraction of an inch to either side, King's aorta would have been punctured, and he would have bled to death in minutes.

Security guards and police had captured the woman who stabbed King, and she was later confined to a mental hospital.

By October, King was well enough to return to Montgomery and relax with his family, which included a second child, Martin Luther King III, who had been born in 1957. However, the terrifying incident in Harlem had created a sense of danger that remained with King throughout his coming triumphs.

King peacefully resisted segregation laws, and his protests often led to his arrest. In 1964, he shared a jail cell with Dr. Ralph Abernathy after their arrest for trespassing in a Florida restaurant. The two ministers had been protesting the policy of segregation in Florida's restaurants.

5

"I Have a Dream"

In 1959, when the SCLC set up its headquarters in Atlanta, King moved there with his family. He joined his father as the copastor of the Ebenezer Baptist Church. Once settled, he organized sit-ins at lunch counters that refused to serve blacks. By the end of 1960, as many as 50,000 blacks were demonstrating at lunch counters all over the South, refusing to give up their seats until they were served. Crowds of angry whites cursed and pushed the protesters, but there was no way to stop them from sitting peacefully at the counters. By the end of the year, 126 towns and cities in the South had integrated their lunch counters and were serving both blacks and whites.

Nineteen sixty was an election year. Senator John F. Kennedy and Vice-president Richard Nixon campaigned for the presidency of the United States. On October 19, three weeks before election day, King and 35 of the 75 black students who accompanied him were arrested for trespassing after staging a sit-in at Rich's department store restaurant in Atlanta. King, who was taken to the Fulton County Jail, refused to post bail (money given for the temporary release of an arrested person; the money is held by a court until the person appears for trial). He said that he would "stay in jail 10 years if necessary." The mayor of Atlanta, who did not want the now-famous King to bring unfavorable publicity to the city, had King released without bail until his trial. A few months before the sit-in, King had been put on probation in DeKalb County, Georgia, for driving with an expired license. The arrest in Atlanta violated King's probation. The DeKalb County sheriff came to Atlanta to arrest King, and a DeKalb judge sentenced him to four months at hard labor in a state prison. The prison, which was at Reidsville, was known for its cruel and harsh treatment of black prisoners.

The presidential candidates were unsure about how to handle King's imprisonment. Nixon stated privately that King was getting a "bum rap," but the candidate said nothing in public. Kennedy also worried that open support of King would anger white voters in the South. However, he did tell his staff members to see what they could do for the jailed civil rights leader. Attorney General Robert Kennedy called the judge in De-Kalb County, and the judge agreed to release King on bail.

King expressed his appreciation to Kennedy, but he did not campaign for either can-

A group of whites in Anniston, Alabama, tries to block a bus carrying Freedom Riders in 1961. The Freedom Riders, a group of blacks and whites, were often the targets of violence during their crusade for integration.

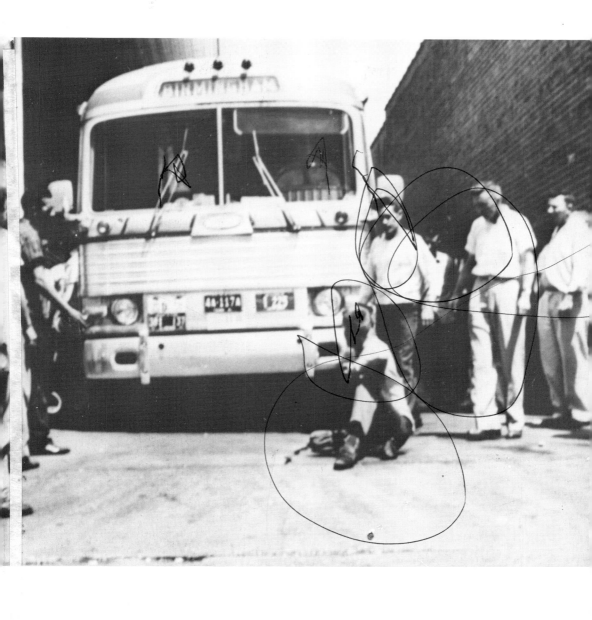

didate. Many black voters were impressed by Kennedy's actions to help King. Blacks in the North voted overwhelmingly for Kennedy, giving him a narrow victory over Nixon.

In October 1961, President Kennedy invited King to the White House. The president told King that he wanted to work to pass civil rights bills but that the southern Democrats in the Congress were powerful enough to keep them from becoming law. King was disappointed but not surprised. He knew that it would take more pressure in the form of marches, sit-ins, and boycotts to win full civil rights for blacks.

Despite earlier rulings by the U.S. Supreme Court that banned segregation in buses, trains, stations, and terminals, many cities in the South continued to segregate. James Farmer, leader of the *Congress of Racial Equality (CORE)*, was determined to force the South into obeying the law. Sponsored by CORE, two groups of blacks and whites boarded buses in Washington, D.C., in May 1961. These groups were known as *Freedom*

Riders. They ignored Whites Only signs as they traveled through Virginia, North Carolina, South Carolina, and Georgia.

At first, white southerners ignored the Freedom Riders. This worried Farmer. He wanted the riders to cause a crisis that would become "headline news all over the world." But the calm ended on May 14, when the Freedom Riders reached Alabama. Outside the town of Anniston, a white mob burned one bus and attacked every Freedom Rider it could find. The second bus went on to Birmingham, where the police allowed members of the Ku Klux Klan to assault the Freedom Riders with lead pipes, baseball bats, and chains for 15 minutes. Finally, Attorney General Robert Kennedy was forced to send 500 U.S. marshals to restore order in Alabama.

The city of Birmingham was strictly segregated, and the police chief, T. Eugene "Bull" Connor, intended to keep it that way. The SCLC faced a difficult task trying to change the attitude of the white citizens. After much prayer, King decided the most effective weapon would be a protest march through the center of the city. On Good Friday, April 12, 1963, 50 marchers led by King and Ralph Abernathy arrived at City Hall. The police arrested them. The hours spent in the city jail were, King later said, the "longest and most frustrating and bewildering hours I have lived." The jailers insulted King and put him alone in a cell without a mattress, pillow, or blanket. They allowed him no visitors or telephone calls. Conditions in the jail improved for King after President Kennedy expressed concern about King's safety. However, King had to remain in jail for eight days, finally gaining his release by paying a $300 fine.

The next day, police with attack dogs and firemen with high-pressure hoses confronted black marchers at Kelly Ingram Park. Powerful streams of water from the fire hoses knocked the blacks to the ground. Unleashed, the police dogs tore the marchers' clothes and skin. Scared and bleeding, the protesters fled.

Pictures of the violence in Birmingham appeared on television and in newspapers all over the country. President Kennedy told some White House visitors that the pictures made him sick. Many Americans had been upset, too, by what they had seen and sent money to the civil rights movement. In Birmingham itself, some white people began to boycott the downtown stores in support of the marchers. Nevertheless, within three days more than 3,000 blacks had been arrested and jailed.

White business leaders, who were losing money because of the boycott, decided to negotiate. The SCLC demanded an end to segregated lunch counters, rest rooms, and drinking fountains; more jobs for blacks; the release of all protesters from jail; and the formation of a committee to work out a plan for continued desegregation.

The business leaders agreed to most of these demands, but other whites were furious. The Ku Klux Klan bombed the home of King's brother,

Alfred, who was also a preacher. Fortunately, no one was home at the time, and there were no injuries. When more acts of violence followed, President Kennedy sent federal troops to Birmingham to stop the attacks.

On June 11, 1963, President Kennedy addressed the nation on television and proposed laws to stop segregation in public buildings and schools. He asked whites to think about how black people were being treated. "Who among us would be content to have the color of his skin changed and stand in his place? Who among us would then be content with the counsels of patience and delay?" He said it was time "for this nation to fulfill its promise of freedom for all citizens."

Encouraged by Kennedy's attitude, King planned a massive civil rights demonstration for Washington, D.C. On August 28, 1963, 250,000 people, both blacks and whites, walked from the Washington Monument to the Lincoln Memorial. As the last speaker of the day, King delivered what may have been his most famous speech. King told his audience and the world, "I have a dream that my four little children will one day live in a nation where they will not be judged by the color of their skin but by the content of their character. . . . And when we allow freedom to ring, when we let it ring from every village and hamlet, from every state and city, we will be able to speed up that day when all of God's children—black men and white men, Jews and Gentiles, Catholics and Protestants—will be able to join hands and to sing in the words of the old Negro spiritual, 'Free at last, free at last; thank God Almighty, we are free at last.'"

More violence came barely three months later, on November 22, 1963. President Kennedy was shot and killed while riding in a motorcade in Dallas, Texas. The nation came to a halt as it mourned the loss of its young leader. When King heard the news, he told Coretta, "I don't think I'm going to live to reach forty. . . . This is what is going to happen to me also. I keep telling you, this is a sick nation. And I don't think I can survive either."

President Lyndon B. Johnson shakes hands with King after signing the Civil Rights Act in 1964. The new law made segregation illegal throughout the United States.

6

"I Have Been to the Mountaintop"

Nineteen sixty-four was a victorious year for King. On July 2, Congress passed a law that ended segregation in public buildings and prohibited employers from practicing racial discrimination. Lyndon B. Johnson, who had become president after the death of John Kennedy, signed the bill into law at a ceremony in the White House. He used 72 pens to sign the bill into law and gave away the pens as souvenirs. Standing behind the president as he signed the bill was Martin Luther King, Jr., who received one of the pens from President Johnson.

In October 1964, King's leadership in the cause of civil rights won him the *Nobel Peace Prize*. This award is given by the government of Norway to the person who has done the most to help achieve world peace. It is considered one of the highest honors in the world. At 35, King was the youngest person ever to receive the award and was the third black.

Family and friends joined Martin and Coretta in Oslo, Norway, where King Olaf V presented the award to King on December 10. When he was given the award, King delivered a speech in which he accepted the award on behalf of the civil rights movement. He also said that the award recognized that nonviolence was the answer to the difficult problems of the time. He gave the $54,000 cash award to the civil rights movement.

The offical end of segregation in the United States still left other problems, such as voting rights. Without being able to choose the people who governed them, blacks could not hope to achieve true equality. Knowing this, white officials in the South still made it very difficult for blacks to register to vote. They demanded that blacks pay a poll tax, and few blacks had the money. Blacks also had to take a literacy test before they could vote. This test might require them to recite a section of the U.S. Constitution or explain a complicated state law, things that very few whites would have been able to do. Thus, only a small percentage of blacks registered to vote. For example, in Selma, Alabama, 15,000 blacks were old enough to vote, but only 383 were able to register.

Local black leaders organized marches to the Selma courthouse to register voters. Selma's sheriff, Jim Clark, did not interfere at first. The next day, however, he ordered the marchers to go home. When they refused, Clark had 226 blacks arrested. The few blacks who had made it into the courthouse and registered soon learned that their applications had been thrown out for some minor reason.

King went to Selma and led another march during which he and 260 followers were arrested. As soon as he was released, he immediately planned a march from Selma to Montgomery, 54 miles away, to present a complaint to the governor of Alabama, George C. Wallace. Governor Wallace, a strict segregationist, ordered the march stopped. When King and his group ignored the order, Alabama state troopers attacked them. Nearly 80 marchers suffered fractured skulls, broken ribs, and various other injuries. That day became known as Bloody Sunday.

On March 15, 1965, President Johnson went before Congress and asked for more powerful voting rights laws, stating that blacks wanted "the full blessings of American life . . . and their cause must be our cause, too." Responding to the president's appeal, Congress passed the Voting Rights Act on August 6, 1965.

In 1966, King began to work on the general problem of poverty. He organized the *Poor People's Campaign*, demanding better homes, schools, and jobs for blacks living in the nation's cities. That summer he went to Chicago to demand the replacement of slums with decent, integrated housing. As King and his supporters marched through an all-white neighborhood, angry crowds threw rocks and bottles at them. King dodged a knife and was later hit by a rock. The marches drew promises of action by Chicago's mayor, but the mayor never followed through, and nothing changed.

Late in 1967, the garbage collectors in Memphis, Tennessee, mostly black men, went on strike for more pay and asked King to help them. On April 3, 1968, King traveled to Memphis. At Mason Temple he gave what later became known as his "I Have Been to the Mountaintop" speech, in which he talked about death. The subject was on his mind because he had been warned that he would be killed in Memphis. In Atlanta, his plane had been searched for a bomb. But he told his audiences that he was not afraid of death "because I have been to the mountaintop. And I've looked over, and I've seen the promised land. . . . I'm not worried about anything. I'm not fearing any man. Mine eyes have seen the glory of the coming of the Lord."

After the speech, King returned to his room at the Lorraine Motel. His brother, Alfred, and a few friends arrived, and the group talked and joked until nearly dawn. Around noon on Thursday, April 4, Ralph Abernathy woke King so they could plan Monday's march in support of the garbage collectors. At 5:00 P.M., King prepared to go to a dinner meeting at Samuel B. Kyle's home with a group of supporters.

King walked out onto the balcony to relax and wait for the others to join him. Suddenly, the evening calm was shattered by the sound of a gunshot. King fell back against the wall, blood spurting from a wound in his neck. His associates rushed out onto the balcony. As Ralph Abernathy bent over the fallen King, trying to revive him, the others frantically pointed to a nearby rooming house where they thought the shot had come from. By the time the police arrived, the gunman had escaped. An ambulance rushed King to a Memphis hospital. He died at the hospital at 7:05 P.M. He was 39 years old.

At the news of King's murder, Americans reacted with shock, grief, and anger. President Johnson proclaimed April 7, 1968, a national day of mourning and ordered all flags to be flown at half-mast.

On April 8, Coretta and her three oldest children, 12-year-old Yolanda, 10-year-old Martin III, and 7-year-old Dexter, led about 20,000 marchers to the city hall in Atlanta as a silent tribute to the fallen leader. (The Kings' youngest child, 5-year-old Bernice Albertine, remained at home.)

King's funeral on April 9 took place at

Ebenezer Baptist Church in Atlanta, where he had been baptized and ordained as a minister. About 800 dignitaries and celebrities joined the King family at the service while millions of Americans watched on television. The service included the playing of a tape recording on which King described what he wished to be said at his funeral. "I don't want a long funeral. . . . [I]f you get somebody to deliver the eulogy [a speech of praise], tell him not to talk too long. Tell him not to mention that I have a Nobel Peace Prize. That isn't important. . . . I'd like someone to mention that day that Martin Luther King, Jr., tried to give his life serving others . . . that I did try to feed the hungry . . . to clothe the naked . . . and to visit those who were in prison. And I want you to say that I tried to love and serve humanity."

King's coffin was placed on an old farm wagon, a symbol of the Poor People's Campaign. Two mules pulled the wagon to the cemetery as 100,000 people slowly marched behind. At the graveside, King's dear friend Ralph Abernathy told the people, "The grave is too narrow for his soul, but we commit his body to the ground."

On King's gravestone are written his name, the dates of his birth and death, and the words from the spiritual song referred to in his "I Have a Dream" speech: "Free at last, free at last, thank God Almighty, I'm free at last."

Meanwhile, a search for the assassin, who had used a .30-06 rifle, had begun. The Federal Bureau of Investigation (FBI) found a fingerprint in the rooming house that they compared to the records of 53,000 known criminals. It matched a print of an escaped convict, James Earl Ray. Two months later, after a worldwide search, Ray was arrested in London, England.

On June 8, 1968, the FBI brought Ray back to Memphis, where he went on trial. At first he pleaded guilty, but Ray later changed his plea to not guilty. The jury convicted Ray of murder, and a judge sentenced him to 99 years in prison. In

On April 9, 1968,
20,000 people followed
King's coffin through
the streets of Atlanta.
His example of peaceful
struggle against injustice
continues to inspire
Americans of all races.

1977, Ray escaped from a maximum-security prison with several other prisoners. The state police began the largest manhunt in Tennessee history. They used 175 people, several helicopters, and bloodhounds to track Ray. They recaptured Ray two days after he escaped.

Martin Luther King, Jr., who was an eloquent speaker, wrote many articles and published six books: *Stride Toward Freedom: The Montgomery Story* (1958); *The Measure of a Man* (1959); *Strength to Love* (1963); *Why We Can't Wait* (1964); *Where Do We Go from Here: Chaos or Community?* (1967); and *The Trumpet of Conscience* (1968).

King's family and friends have not allowed his beliefs, accomplishments, and nonviolent methods to die with him. They have created a living memorial to him in Atlanta, Georgia—the Martin Luther King, Jr., Center for Nonviolent Social Change. The organization is dedicated to eliminating worldwide poverty, racism, ignorance, violence, and war.

Americans remember Martin Luther King, Jr., each year on the third Monday of January with a national holiday celebrating his birthday. Martin Luther King Day is the first national holiday to honor an individual black American.

Further Reading

Other Biographies of Martin Luther King, Jr.

Bains, Rae. *Martin Luther King*. Mahwah, NJ: Troll, 1985.

Davidson, Margaret. *I Have a Dream: The Story of Martin Luther King*. New York: Scholastic, 1986.

McKissack, Patricia. *Martin Luther King, Jr.: A Man to Remember*. Chicago: Children's Press, 1984.

Milton, Joyce. *Marching to Freedom: The Story of Martin Luther King, Jr.* New York: Dell, 1987.

Related Books

Berry, Joy. *Every Kid's Guide to Understanding Human Rights*. Chicago: Children's Press, 1987.

Greenfield, Eloise. *Rosa Parks*. New York: HarperCollins, 1973.

Chronology

Jan. 15, 1929   Martin Luther King, Jr., is born
in Atlanta, Georgia.

1948   Graduates from Morehouse College and
is ordained a Baptist minister; enters
Crozer Theological Seminary.

1953   Marries Coretta Scott in Marion,
Alabama.

1954   Becomes pastor of the Dexter Avenue
Baptist Church in Montgomery,
Alabama.

1955   Receives Ph.D. from Boston University;
joins bus boycott after Rosa Parks
is arrested; becomes president of
the Montgomery Improvement Association (MIA).

1956   U.S. Supreme Court declares segregation
on buses unconstitutional.

1957   King creates the Southern Christian
Leadership Conference (SCLC); leads the

Prayer Pilgrimage for Freedom in Washington, D.C.

1958 *Stride Toward Freedom: The Montgomery Story* is published; King stabbed in New York City.

1959 Becomes copastor of the Ebenezer Baptist Church; imprisoned in Reidsville, Georgia.

1963 In April, leads protest march in Birmingham, Alabama; on August 28, he delivers speech at March on Washington; on November 22, President Kennedy is shot and killed in Dallas, Texas.

1964 King wins the Nobel Peace Prize.

1966 Organizes the Poor People's Campaign.

April 4, 1968 King is shot and killed in Memphis, Tennessee.

Glossary

boycott   an act of protest in which a group of people stop buying from or dealing with a store or company in order to obtain certain demands

civil rights   the personal and property rights of a person, recognized by a government and guaranteed by a constitution and its laws

Congress of Racial Equality (CORE)   a group dedicated to fighting segregation that sponsored the Freedom Riders bus ride through the South in 1961

discrimination   the unfair treatment of an individual, group, or race

Freedom Riders   groups of blacks and whites from Washington, D.C., who traveled through the South in 1961 to protest segregation

Great Depression   a period of time during the 1930s when many businesses closed, the unemployment rate was high, and many people were poor

Jim Crow   a character from minstrel shows during the 19th century; Jim Crow became another term for racial discrimination

Ku Klux Klan   a secret, all-white society whose members believe in the supremacy of the white race

National Association for the Advancement of Colored People (NAACP)   organization founded in 1909 that challenged segregation and discrimination

Nobel Peace Prize   an award given by Norway to a person or group of persons who have done much work toward achieving world peace

nonviolence   a form of protesting without using physical force to obtain certain goals, such as equal treatment or government assistance

Poor People's Campaign   an organization founded by Martin Luther King, Jr., to help blacks in cities find better homes, schools, and jobs

protest   an act of complaint or display of objection to an idea

segregation   the policy of separating members of a certain group or race from a main body or group

sermon   a speech for religious teaching given by a priest or minister as part of a religious service

Southern Christian Leadership Conference (SCLC)   a group started by Martin Luther King, Jr., that protested segregation by nonviolent actions

Index

Kathy Kristensen Lambert grew up in the San Francisco Bay area. She received her A.A. degree from the College of Marin and her B.A. in elementary and business education from the University of Washington. Mrs. Lambert teaches fifth grade in the Monroe School District of Washington State. She lives in Redmond, Washington, with her husband, Daryl, and her two children, Char and Craig.

Picture Credits

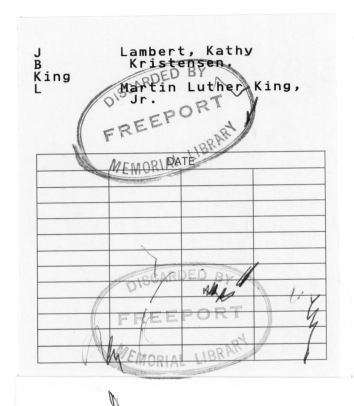

J
B
King
L

Lambert, Kathy
Kristensen.
Martin Luther King,
Jr.

		DATE	